THE
EVE
RY
DAY
WIF
E

modjaji books

THE EVERYDAY WIFE

Phillippa Yaa de Villiers

Publication © Modjaji Books 2010

Text © Phillippa Yaa de Villiers 2010

First published in 2010 by Modjaji Books CC

P O Box 385, Athlone, 7760, South Africa

http://modjaji.book.co.za

www.modjajibooks.co.za

ISBN 9781920397050

Book and cover design: Jacqui Stecher

Cover photograph: Victor Dlamini

Printed and bound by Harbec Packaging

Set in Palatino

For Pervaiz, with thanks for opening the library of your heart
For Felix, my anchor, the fire to which I always return

Foreword

What treats are served up in this new book of poems by Phillippa Yaa de Villiers!

To read just the first line of the first poem is to be skeined into a tantalizing world where nothing is predictable. Like the best of poets, she makes language do her bidding, wresting new sense from familiar images and situations, surprising us and ambushing our expectation. In the title poem can be seen the range and subtlety that characterises her work – the clear-eyed honesty, the perceptiveness, the playfulness, the attention to nuance. *'The Everyday Wife'* sums up the boundaries and expanses of a relationship, the possibility of menace, even, in the midst of love.

In one way or another, Phillippa Yaa de Villiers illuminates relationships of many kinds and many intensities – between lovers, children and parents, the politics of emotion shared and remembered and confronted, sustained across the distance of place or memory. Sometimes, as in *'The Organ of Love'* - which manages that crucial combination of passion and humour – she makes meaning hold on to the last word of the poem like the last drop of a delicious drink.

In poem after poem are revealed different facets of her shapeshifting talent. The raw and numbing truths told in *'Hell in a Handbag'* contrast starkly with the theatricality of a supermarket encounter in *'The Middle Promise'*, which transforms into a reminder that *'the cost of things is not the same as the value of things'*.

The historical and everyday realities of South Africa permeate even her observations about the weather as in *'Home drenched'* or *'Dictatorship'*, and in *'Sixty-nine bullets'* (for the Sharpeville 69) the tragedy is given poignant new impact.

Her blending of the literal and the metaphysical makes it possible to take so much from a single image:

one girl
sits tidily beside a giant cactus, the giant sun
just another father: distant and a little too warm.

The alarming familiar that she summons up so matter-of-factly, and so well, in *'The guest'* epitomizes that edginess of imagination, and the sanity of the conclusion that one can never improve on freedom.

Phillippa Yaa de Villiers has claimed a freedom to speak the unspoken, however it emerges.

'A safe house is a place of fear' – a title thought-provoking in itself - captures the potency of silence, the dangerous power of wordlessless, where *'silence is the skin of fear'*.

'Words become me,' she begins by saying, in *'Lasso'*…*'without them I am shorn'*. Phillippa Yaa de Villiers is a poet for whom there is no danger of separation from expression. She definitely has a way with words, and words have their way with her.

MARGARET BUSBY
OBE
NANA AKUA ACKON 1

Contents

Part 1

Part 2

Part 3

Part 4

Lasso

Words become me.
They are the flowers in my hair,
jewels at my neck and ears.

Words adorn my being.
without them I am shorn,
grey as a corpse,
silent as the stinging rain,
beggared by forces too big to conquer,
too unnameable to tame.

Beyond the fence
wild words gallop free,
yet to be harnessed to my plough.
And those are the ones
most beautiful to me:

I want to be a cowgirl with a noose
lassoing wild words
and in my own field
setting them loose.

Chinatown

Each time I blow the embers of desire
a tiny flame leaps up and
ignites my body. I am
a piece of land,
master of a burning estate

with no water in sight.

Sometimes it lights a fuse
to a thick pile of red firecrackers
and then we're in Chinatown again, with its
warm beer and perfect children and I am a noisy dragon
and I explode
in bright light, scare dogs
and small children.

Or I am a catherine wheel
I spin round and round and round
in the black night
till I'm spent.

In the morning
they sweep the empty cartridges:
the husks of screams,
used delight
piled up next to the wheelie bin.

Stolen rivers

For Chiwoniso Maraire

We Africans came to Berlin to sing
and recite poetry. We had an agenda:
remembering our anthems of loss,
galloping, consuming,
the pillage, the cries
like forest fires, like haunted children,
how can we, how can we even
begin to redress?
Enraged, we wanted revenge
and then, Chiwoniso, you stepped on the stage and
you opened your mouth and
every stolen river of platinum and gold
poured out of your mouth in song;
your voice etched us out of the night
and doubled the light in each of us.
You restored all the treasure-houses
from Benin to Zimbabwe, Mapungubwe to Cairo;
Africa moved its golden bones,
shook off its heavy chains
and danced again.
That night I thought
if only
love could purchase bread,
Africans would not be hungry.

Envy

I envy women
with the clean envelope
of their pleated sex
unwritten on.
No acrid spill of ink to
interrupt the smooth serenity
of their being, flowing without interference
into the eternity of their imagination.
Behind their curtain of conformity
they spin their continuity,
embroider their stories
on walls of crisp linen,
weave blankets of homilies,
comforted by repetition.
Safe.
This is their time:
they will step on to the stage of this
enamoured century, like
a missing actor coming to take her place.
Her big night is here.
We, the incoherent
watch from the wings.

The everyday wife

Lover, you hold me
in the palm of your hand,
I lie in your pocket.
I am small change.
You spend me without thinking.
You will always have me.
You do not have to save me.
I am like
an everyday wife.

If we get committed we'll probably go insane,
sweet nothings will become bitterly inane,
bond becomes mortgage, lead-lined shoes
vows repeated solemnly, death by noose.

I think we should rather
stay loose.

Night-fishing with Daddy

We turn off the national road, bump-bump-
bumping through the veld, till we arrive at
the great wet eye of the dam. The sun is low
but it's still light. We unpack the truck. I've
brought a friend along, she's thirteen to my
aspirant twelve. While daddy puts up the tent,
we play shyly around the water's edge. She's
Italian, not used to camping or the outdoors.
Her brand new tackies sparkle against the wild
grasses. Two boys swim across the dam to talk
to us. They ask us if we are models. My eyes
are full of my friend: she's so sophisticated,
the way she laughs at boys. Daddy prepares
the rods and the bait. I am self-conscious. I
don't want her to see how expertly I can hook
a worm. Our favourite fish are sweet-fleshed
kurper and carp. We use worms for carp.
Kurper prefer lumps of bread or mielie pap
flavoured with custard powder or curry. We
grasp the rods and follow daddy's movement,
and cast. Listen to the long song of the line
as it flies over the water, then the plop as the
bait-laden hooks hit the water, and we girls
giggling. Three times: song, plop, giggle,

song plop giggle

song   plop   giggle.

Daddy lights the lantern. Boredom nibbles at our minds.
A wild bird bustles noisily through the reeds, finding
its nest. I steal a look at my friend. She sits passively as
the shadows come to lie around her like old pets. I am
mortified: she must be hating this. Teenagers should not
be forced to go fishing. Worm-like I resent, struggling
against the hook; finally, I resign myself:

surrender to night

wait to see what the water

will return to us.

Origin

Tonight,
my son, my favourite poem,
shares my bed.
His gentle snores like footprints on the night.
He is upside down. What dream
is holding him
by the ankle?

It has been two weeks and 10 000 miles,
our skins and eyes separated from one another.
Mothers and their sons inhabit each other differently.
We are more than milk; we are also
bread and the law and desire.
I know that
I am his home, as much as he is
my shelter. I am an expanding house,
growing taller as he reaches past me for
his own life.

Che Guevara changed the world for me. He was
some mother's son who dreamt a fairer future.
Our breakfast is our ideals, what we want
the world to be, most important of the
meals; and life, the greatest prize, we fight
in trenches to defend its sovereignty.
This is how I was born in blood and
pain and mortality, my mind bright,
laughing up to wish for more, and force
my tired feet against the discouraged hill,
and harness my rage and ride it home to change,
and still return to that first poem that called me
Mama.

Getting to know yourself in Amsterdam museums

I

It is spring in Amsterdam.
We can hear the earth breathing, wearing
strings of tulips at her breast. Deep inside, the turning
of uncountable colours of humanity, their sexes and their dreams.

(The dream was like an arrow and the arrow flew out of the swamp,
out of the muddy brown water, and into the sky, pulling the sky
open like a wound behind it. In the open wound of sky, angels were
suddenly revealed, going about their angel business in their usual
way. Angels pumping up bicycle tyres, pumping iron, pumping their
muscles, angels all encased in perfect skin that ranged from darkest
ebony to milk, like the Paul Simon song, angels with perfect bodies
and perfect teeth and perfect eyes and the sweet sensation of their
collective beauty intoxicates us and we yell out: 'Hallelujah! Amen!'
and for that moment we speak in parables of Paradise.
You can see it in the streets, the people pressing onward to the next
revelation, their wheels spinning as they ride, joy in their eyes, Amen
for Amsterdam and her peddled dreams.
Then all the parables are strung together as waist beads for a dancer,
there are no wasted beats, her firm, heavy breasts have a sheen of
sweat, moonlight reflects off her like silver, like a lightning ricochet,
and it surrounds her as she arches her back and stamps her feet and
shakes her body in ecstasy, and the energy leaps off her skin in sparks
that ignite the thatch roof in flames, and then the village is burnt
down, we will never be able to return, oh, oh, oh no, I've got the blues
again, the night opens like a shout, like an empty gourd, like a belly
birthed of its young, and all of the nights, all of the paradises are her
children, and her name is rhythm and she is actually God.)

II The Vincent Van Gogh Museum
In this temple to the patron poet of Dutch creativity Saint Vincent,
we look with reverence at all the stories that
he left behind. The silence of the women billows out of the walls
in delicate colours carefully mixed and chosen by the master;
light speaks in strident stripes but what does light have to say besides
I am here! What does light have to hide…

The mirrors reflect bourgeois comforts:
a man with his books, a woman with her piano;
not the urgent press
of blade against flesh,
bodies pushed by pain to the border
of endurance, then
exiled, beyond words, to the agony
of torn-out roots, chopped
limbs, the new fuel for the sugar harvest,
wealth against poverty: black against white.

III
If I were an academic, I would write about systematic cruelty.
I would be able to argue, through references,
that the pain Vincent felt was not the same
as the nameless slaves felt, and that even though
he was not acknowledged in his lifetime,
neither were they.

IV
Some see God in their own image
and others see God as a woman with a pitful of snakes at her feet
and others see God as a monkey, others as an elephant.
When you look in the mirror, what do you see?

The Tropenmuseum

V Erzulie Freda
God is a blueblind baby
with eyes smeared by love, beaten child
unconditionally attached. Plastic serenity
in her round cheeks, innocent as
a knife, as a disease. She is always with us.
Always and forever. She'll carry our butterfly prayers
in her fat little hands, sometimes squeezing them a little too hard
out of curiosity. And our prayers, which are rather resilient,
will stretch their wings against her infant vitality.

VI Erzulie Danthor
Nail the lips shut.
Pound the eyes until nothing remains but pools of blood.
There are no rules
in cruelty that pushes the flesh to
submit in echoes of ecstasy (it's easier once you let go).

He wanted to see her split; the moment that her eyes reflected
the pain that her body felt. This is the passion, like Christ,
like a virgin kiss with wet euphemisms and rock hard conviction;
all over the world fear tortures life,
'I am right' rapes the please, don't so many times
that in the climax, neither knows who is who, and nobody cares
because the victim is almost dead.

VII Image
You may look
but you may not touch;
you may not nail it
or throw chicken blood on it
or egg.
This is a god under guard,
polite, civilized.

Crows in a wheatfield:
the earth of optimistic light
is covered with scavengers
fragments of night.

Voodoo goes to the darkest human deeds
and holds them, trembling, to the light
covered in blood and sputum.

This is the altar where we pray
to what we fear most: our ability to destroy
and our sacred task to make ourselves
whole again.

I want god as close to me as the dishwashing liquid
and as affordable as toilet paper,
because I need her frequently and I need him
at every meal and if you follow your darkness
to the border, where the language falters and your
sense is reduced to shrieks of agony,
you will be able to hear nothing but a heartbeat
as you did when you forced yourself
into the world. Nothing but the pressing walls of muscle
that birthed you in blood and flesh. Son of man, daughter of god
can you see yourself now?

In the red

When you've had a suicide
in the family,
you should probably not spend
too long looking into it.
You should avoid time
at the mirror
peering below the surface.
Rather don't wonder what it means
to convince yourself, and then
make a commitment.
Suicide is all about conviction and
cutting: sentences like
'He was always unhappy, anyway'.
To 'he was always'.
To 'he was'.
Finally
the bankrupt
'he'.

I avoid spending,
try to save myself,
calculate how much pain
he must have felt
against how much he left.

Fifteen years later
I am still in the red.

Tissue paper

When I go to the metropole I feel defensive:
We Africans are not barbaric, I assert.
Meanwhile the TV yells
that we have elected
an alleged rapist
an accused thief
an unashamed polygamist
to the presidency.

I tell them they don't know what it's like:
there are differences in custom and tradition,
loss happens in translation,
these things are also coloured by racism
the west has its pets, its tame Annans,
it's not our fault that you don't understand us –
you never have.

On the flight home, I study the cold
black tablet of the aeroplane window.
Level with the stars, we cruise over Africa
her masses in their thrall of poverty,
their unnegotiated fate.

When I step off the plane, I feel like a missionary.
I want to tell everybody to use a condom,
treat women fairly, get educated, get a life.

Travelling pulls me apart
into soft tissue paper
in layers;
I wouldn't have it any other way.

It's so much easier
to pack the fragile things.

What the dead say

Cities stand
like ravished women
called Maputo, Accra, Mombasa;
on a beach of bleached
memory.

Torn, shattered, only half-
decent, with that lewd, innocent look around the eyes
that girls get when they've been used too soon:
they know how to please and how to get
what they need. They watch sailors come
and go.

The waves blow the mind
back to the first sharp pain as
hard men forced themselves in
and buildings bled history
into the soil of time. Now a tattered
cover-girl seduces
visitors to exotic destinations while
the dead walk the streets,

their last cries woven into the bricks of its fortresses:
'We have no place in this history they say
is ours. Who are these heroes? Strangers stare
out of books
like products in foreign shop windows. Please,
please show me a picture of me,
tell my story.'

Hell in a handbag

My mother's handbag
matched her earrings, matched
her shoes.
From time to time she lectured me
on universal truths.

Truth Number One: your body
is a temple. And matching clothes impose
a doctrine –
organized religion.

Truth Number Two: a woman
always knows.
Aloud I wondered what the hell that meant.
Impatiently, (her pocket vanity
reflecting puckered lipstick narcissistic),
she replied: you'll understand
when you grow up.

Truth Number Three: it's she
who decides, the woman. Only,
power – like perfume – should be sensed
rather than smelled. She powdered
her nose
and said –

Truth Number Four: discretion
is the better part of virginity. Ladies know
a secret is a weapon.

So   I   told   her   one.

Truth
Number
Five: mother,
at six years old I was raped.

Her blue eyes wide, she replied: that's
terrible, dear.
Then:
it's happened to all of us, my child.
We must throw it in the dustbin
and only keep the good memories.
we must move on, move on.

Truth Number Six: we didn't
speak about it again. It became
an accident, and
talking tore open the dustbin to reveal
the mess of broken flesh
the chaos of emergency
the onlookers faces painted blueredyellowwhite
by the ambulance lights -
complexions bruised by curiosity.

Truthnumberseven: at eighteen I fell
pregnant.
She said to me
regretfully:
you've lost your innocence.

And I replied:
save it for the deathbed, darling.
This woman knows
that innocence
has gone to hell in a handbag –
matching dustbin, matching earrings, matching
silence.

Lips painted shut.
Pain blown into a discreet tissue and discarded like mucus.
I have knelt at mother's knee
imbibing certainty, like milk,
and the Milky Way has gone sour
because of universal truths.

Truth Number Eight: I have grown and now I know
that power – unlike perfume –
is only power when it's felt.
A smashed bottle on the bathroom floor
is not the sweet sense of surrender,
but a broken child who was never held.

The truth is not a token:
I've set fire to the temple,
the flames shout out in tongues
the words you left unspoken.

Cirque ordinateur

Every night is the same:
writers sit at computers
and dream…

I climb to the highest ladder
of the chapiteau and fly:
Le public echoes the sigh
of the village I lost.
Later the ringmaster strips his mime
and licks her summer thighs right down
to her feet,
and tells me to piss off in Russian.
I scuttle into midnight.

The radio is on in nomad's land
and I am receiving five frequencies,
the caravans are closed   *les caravanes sont fermées,*
the moon opens itself up to dreams   *la lune s'ouvre aux reves,*
the Mongolians are fighting again
they always drink too much on Friday
the German dwarf lost all his money   *le nain allemand hat al sein*
Gelt gelassen,
gambled it at the casino.

These are my people:

with each swing of the trapeze,
I come home and leave,
dancing and traveling with writers
tapping at the keyboard of memories.

Eating times two

Hunger grumbles,
fragrant food seduces
the stomach
rumbles;
our eyes journey to the Sunday chicken,
genteel lips conceal gushing saliva,
we look away to pray,
amen gives way
to flashing knives and mashing teeth:
for now, hunger retreats.

The tourist asks
why Africa is hungry.
Divided the heart:
we don't know how to answer.

Outside
hunger humbles,
a beggar reaches into
the cold skies of a stranger's eyes
as hunger tumbles
hope
into a gutter of stuttering
half-baked dreams
and aborted fantasies
and bungles plans
and scrambles opportunities,
and hunger stumbles
along blocked synapses,
bumps its head repeatedly as

bulimic greed
dry heaves
its simulated grief,
stuffing images of lust
into a seething cavity
of need.

The tourist asks
how we plan
to solve the problem.
Subtracted the stomach:
we don't know how to answer.

Hard-working
hunger, the farmer
sows rows of skeletons,
and waits for an empty harvest.
Hunger builds a boat of bones,
casts a net of starving eyes,
people drown in dust, without resisting.
There is no second course;
dying fragments loaf
along the desert's shore.

The tourist is the authority.
They know how to stay alive! We are still learning.
Politely we wipe our mouths and give thanks for what we
have
received: pronunciation, and chicken, on Sundays.
Contradiction multiplied:
we don't know how to answer.

We live by killing,
we can't explain.
Perhaps hunger will come
to our table one day;
by then, most probably,
the tourist will have
gone away.

Love at a distance: a cycle for America

I Katrina

A cyclone is decapitating the houses
the air is full of flailing roofs, the streets are waterlogged
and politicians are at loggerheads: figureheads on a ship
that's run aground zero. Here lies the soul of our distant
civilization, replaying insanity day by daytime reruns of
the drama of despair, the theatre of confusion,
while we try to find the centre, turn our good ear
to the ground to hear the whole truth
unburdened by fear. Embedded storytellers
have kept us dumb and innocent
and the centre is nowhere near,
it is buried
deep in the heart of each of us,
wherever that is, and even though I know that
I can't understand why
I burnt another dinner tonight:
such a simple thing to get right.

II Response Ability
A mandate is a line of dead summers in the
graveyard of the nation's memory. All that green.
Saplings chopped down by an axe-wielding icon,
a cut-out dictator with double-barrelled eyes.
From Vietnam to Afghanistan and all the wars between, lies
that were told are retold; and those raised on grits and those
who sell grit bit down on the nothing that they inherited, and then
the impossible happened; hope took a look in the mirror
before stepping out on the balcony and singing a love song
to a beaten, exhausted world. No matter where you come from
a silenced heart is only one thing: dead. And when we heard his voice
we woke up in his smile and with both hands
gave him power.

III Holding

The squeal of tyres receding into the
morning is now a memory, or a mirage:
each time she moves towards it, it dissolves.
The cross country road movie beauty pageant carnival
of politics left some time ago, and now one girl
sits tidily beside a giant cactus, the giant sun
just another father: distant and a little too warm.
It is very quiet. Her heart throbs simply like breath;
he was almost here. Almost.
His brown hands close, a father she could touch.
She wonders how it would be if he held her.
She in her little cage of fear, wild small
animal unable to trust, and he reaches for her and she
bares her teeth and snaps at him, watches him withdraw
his hurt fingers. She licks his blood from her teeth.
He'd better not disappoint. She hopes he will try again.
He won't be like all the others. But hope tastes like dust these days,
she thinks as she reaches for her last cup of water, as tanks
roll across other deserts, and buried people cry for their lives.

The dark around my neck

When we started it was just getting dark.
Your face was a flame and I wanted to cup it,
to keep it, to light my way up the mountain.
We were sitting close to a small fire, we had eaten
and washed our dishes and we were resting before
continuing our walk.
Your eyes were setting on my face,
stroking me with a warm light; behind me the moon was rising,
I could almost lean on it.
Around us the darkness was settling like a big
black dog, turning and turning in his night basket,
only his crickets creaking.

It was clear, but mountains are unpredictable:
sometimes without any warning, a mist seems to
percolate from the dreaming earth, and then
it becomes dangerous,
you could fall.
As night shawled the cooling
shoulders of rocks
we stood up
and stamped out the fire;
and picked up our bags
and stepped on to the path.

This how we are: each takes their own bag and
continues their lonely ascent;
neither will carry the other's burden.
Although we were now physically separated,
we still touched one another with our voices,
until our words fell behind us
like dew
sinking into silence.
Our feet carried on talking
in the stone language of the path. I could see you up ahead,
the late crescent moon over your shoulder, the stars
holding hands across millions of light years
as we entered the immense embracing dark.
As you disappeared I tried to keep the light you carry
inside you and I tried to hear your feet speak
but my ears were deaf to all but the sound of my own exertion.

Now the dark is around my neck.
I am terrified; alone and lonely.
I shout once, just to hear another voice.
There is no reply:
only an echo.

I thought of my son,
our daily return to the hearth of his origin: my lap.
The busy day coils up its hands at eight,
our breasts breathe together, and
I give to him the candle of my eyes
and kiss him warm to keep out the damp and lonely mist.
He sets off on his night voyage
in his single bed.

I exhale and breathe again.

I know that somewhere on this mountain, you too
are walking and maybe wondering where
the flame of my face has gone
and the path pulls you on and you may not wait
and you startle a nightjar,
it flaps off to the left, and you pause and listen,
you cling to the path, the narrow throat of the bulk that holds us
with its necklace of unremarkable stones,
we the children, the mountain our mother.
I know that on this mountain you are walking just as I
am walking and I want to hold your face between my hands again
and know the way. There is only one certainty: the path,
and all I want is to believe that
when the dawn calls out life, I will see you

and we will come together like this landscape
passive and natural
without fear
about to be discovered.

Problem child

Johannesburg was a baby
born with teeth
that bit the midwife
as it struggled to light.

A thousand people heard her scream
and walked across moons to find
what lay beyond the known fields
of their dismembered history.

They are still waiting
to find what gold tastes like.

Faithful as a shadow

You are carried by your story until you are big enough to walk.
Then it adjusts its steps to walk beside your little feet
as you begin your journeys of discovery,
green and curious, growing everywhere.
When your small hand tears a flower to pieces
or you burn yourself on a hot iron
the story goes deeper, grows deeper.
You become taller and defiant:
your fast legs outrun your story as you tell yourself
another story, making your own story
by resisting the story you were given.
But the story is faithful as a shadow, it will not leave,
even if you put on the loudest music
to drown the story's insistent waterfall voice
it will drip into your ear and
build a dam in your brain.
You cannot shut it out.
Because when the party is over
you will find a puddle on the dance floor.
You will switch on the light and look up.
And there will be
no sign of a leak.

The story will make itself into any form to get intimate with you.
On a night of loss, your body will reach out and find
a subtle pulse of hope: your story sleeping beside it.
When you wake up in the morning, your story shakes out the sheets.
One day you will thank your story for always being with you:
as witness, companion and shelter,
curving like a river through all the landscapes
of your life, sustaining you with its water,
making and marking your earth.
Even death will not separate you, for then
your story will continue in the mouths of others.

Your life is a world
that you honour
by giving it a voice.

The Middle Promise

I like to look at men;
yesterday at the Gem superstore
I gave the elegant Somali in the next queue
a long, smouldering up-and-down
with lots of lashes.
Like a pirate I swung on to
his clean brown deck,
and his coffee eyes
poured right through me.
I was nothing more
than a vessel
on the ocean of
Sunday afternoon:
becalmed in the
middle of the room,
almost invisible.

My womb turns restlessly in its warm belly.
A slight but significant ache. I count my periods.
My eggs are all but spent. I can still hear
the music of sex, but I am no longer in the dance.
I am a walled, empty temple
where silence flowers.

In the beginning we are promised nothing but
the firm hunger of our perfect bodies, and
at the end, the aches, the dreams of bones,
mortal wisdom as a final breath,
the gift of living to the gifted dead.

This middle seems so promiseless –
yet
we have learned that
the cost of things is not the same
as the value of things; having tasted loss
we ask for more,
we calibrate minutes in love, degrees in uncertainty,
our voices grow stronger as our bodies fade.

The other day they found a buried city, thousands of years old.
In the kitchen place, an unbroken clay pot, its whole body held in the silt-
ing earth.
We are aging vessels, dug up to face the light.
Unbroken.
Still useful.
Filled with stories.

Dismissed

I feel dismissed by you like a private.
You are a corporal looking at me in disgust.
'You're so pathetic. Why don't you just go home to mother?'

If only you knew, corporal,
that when the private gets home, he finds
his mother passed out
at the kitchen table,
her wrinkled reptile temple pressed
against the red formica, empty beer bottles
all around. He's seen this all before,
he knows what to do.

He steps neatly around her.
Starts picking up the mess – she has spilt the dog food again.
Like a husband he puts his arm around her shoulder
and pulls her to her feet. Her head
falls forward sharply.
He gentles her with soft words
and kneels at her feet in the dark toilet as he prepares her
for bed. It's all right Mum, he says as
he lays her out on the green bedspread and takes off her shoes.
He stops then, sits on the edge of the bed

with the darkness lapping at his feet,
remembering himself:
a small boy in shorts
framed by his mother's snores -

so don't imagine that I'm afraid or humiliated
when you tell me to run home to mother.

Unfinished business

The city writes itself behind my eyelids as I sleep.
The lines of traffic like an alphabet of ambition;
it lays down a grid pattern of goals, and for a brief time
we know where we are going. In the no-man's land
abandoned developments lie with their legs spread
like drunkards caught by the morning light.

Going down there

This is a letter scratched out by candlelight:
I leave it for all those who are also
confined, painfully pressed, split open.
Those who hold themselves tightly in their hands
so that they will not spill over
and drain away.
Fear eats hope like the night eats the day
leaving only crumbs of stars. Too far away
to be of any help.

I was raped at six, 11, at 13, at 17 and 19
I didn't know I was violated because
where I came from
love was forced and
sometimes hurt.

The frail meat of humankind
can't withstand extremes. We construct ourselves
around ourselves, making of our lives
a shelter.
When you build a house,
you place the window carefully;
when you grow out of a wound,
you see life through
a survivor's eyes.

Rapes were my bread: I eat   I understand.
Then later;   I understand,   I eat.
The marks on my house / body / shell are
the keloid memories of
African warriors: scars
deliberately inflicted, a sign of identity.
I read them like Braille.

When they found me I was filthy,
wild and mute. They asked me: what
happened? Compassion unlocked
the cage of memory, and words fell out of me
like the crumbs in Gretel's dark forest,
pebbles of hope,
words
became light
showing me
how to get home.

I am healed now.
But I no longer
look the same.

A safe house is a place of fear

7 July 2005

We've been gathering silences again:
you and me, chasing thoughts down holes, and then
stuffing them with non-committal commentary.
Passion doused by the slow porridge of domesticity.

Words fail to cross the thick air between us.
They fall onto the floor and are sucked up
by the vacuum of silence in this ice-white room.
The half-spoken sentence,
the luminous thought,
the buried retort:
all woven to nothing on apathy's loom:
and
this
parched
moment
ticks
in the
anonymous
rucksack
of another
quiet
evening at home.

I shoulder it carefully, not wanting to rupture
the fragile balance of civility.

Light-years away, behind thick glass:
murder is devised
and televised.
Unedited London trembles and bleeds
in technicolour emotions that spill out and are absorbed
by the living-room carpet.

Here silence is the skin of fear:
bombs explode through
the wound
the chaos
the tear.

Sixty-nine bullets

(for the Sharpeville 69)

Sixty-nine bodies
caught in half-sentences:

- I was on my way to the shop
- I saw this chap I like
- He's all fire, his skin and eyes
- Are copper weapons, blazing in the turning sun
- I go soft in his hard eyes, can't stop smiling
- Oh, it was still quiet when I came past
- And he told me to go home
- Things could get nasty
- Then he smiled and said
- Let's meet
- Afterwards
- I didn't know the protest was illegal
- But I suppose that's obvious, after all
- Isn't everything we blacks do
- Illegal?
- I tried to get in front of her
- But it was too late
- She fell first
- I didn't want to be a voiceless victim
- I knew exactly what I was getting into
- But she was not supposed to be there
- I was escorting my friend
- He is into this PAC
- My father says we should rather get better jobs than he could

- Who wants to be a matshingilane in Hillbrow
- Some blacks are even lawyers, he says. Why do I pay school fees?
- I told him, this protest is for him too
- He said he's on night shift, he hasn't got time for
- This young boy's nonsense
- He couldn't see his way to be there,
- So I was there for him.
- Me, I was clear in my mind,
- Because I was nineteen
- Robert Sobukwe spoke at our school
- We can only liberate ourselves and it starts here
- It was true, why are we poor tenants of our own
- Inheritance?
- This disorder could only be cured
- By naming it, and inhibiting its spread
- By liberating our minds from its poison
- Hey, death happens to everyone
- We should not take it personally, after all, it was a protest,
- It was political
- We knew what we were doing,
- What is this world we are creating?
- Rather die for freedom than live like a slave
- What will I tell my children when they ask

- Where were you?
- Whatever happens, at least I spoke out
- It was political, I agree
- But death is personal
- Very personal
- Each death as unique as birth
- With its own portents
- And banalities
- Who will fetch the baby from the crèche?
- Who will tell my mother?
- I didn't mean to hurt
- I didn't know what we were doing was so bad
- Oh well, we knew we were risking
- But still
- All my tomorrows
- All my tomorrows, please
- I surrender
- I surrender
- I surrender
- I surrender
- Please, could you stop shooting
- Now?

Jozi parks

Smashed beer bottles don't give a damn
about barefoot children. Adults, swollen
with disappointment, sit sadly in the swings.
They've got their own problems: they are empty now
and useless; most of the time, shattered and discarded.
Children come uninvited, so let them cut their feet:
we all learn through pain. We were the same.
They'll grow up make the same mistakes
that we did again.
Our parents also saved up and bought us shoes
and still we limp home.

Home drenched

We South Africans rarely
discuss the weather.
Temperature, yes, the highs and lows
of daily fluctuations, talked out in seams of
exhaled complaints. But not
the weather.
Its ordinary wisdom is never analyzed.
We are trained by the glib
sunshine
to forgive too easily, we slide into optimism
as into a well-fitting trouser.

So when the storm comes we don't have an umbrella.

And it comes unexpectedly: we admire the mass movement
of the stately cumulus, their darkening
from cream to
bilious purple pent-up rage.
Snake-tongue lightning licking the rooftops
streets awash with revenge
cars skidding over the unstable firmament
hail hurled in furious stones .

We are terminally surprised
when we get home,
drenched. I had no idea, we say
that you were so angry.

The guest

My best room contains a bed,
a pile of books;
the sunshine comes in.
I like lying in it
and dreaming
and reading
and writing.

Then one day I got a visitor.
A dark stranger
stood framed in the blue rectangle of the doorway
with two creatures at his feet; one with three heads,
the other whining, its jaws dripping pools
of mucus mixed with blood.

Is it sick? I asked.
He nodded. His eyes were empty and desperate.
We're hungry and we need to rest
please:

What's your name? I asked.
He said with a paranoid giggle that he could only tell me
if I promised not to tell
anyone else.

Kensington's full of loonies, sometimes they wander
along the koppie to Troyeville;
so I closed the door behind me and stood
outside with him in the sun.
Those things at his feet, those
matted creatures growled and snarled and whined and
he made no attempt to control them
until the three-headed one bit me on the ankle
and he kicked it and said:
they're fine when they get to know you.

He said I know you.
I've been watching you.
And I've seen you've got no-one.
Sometimes you're so lonely that
you talk to yourself,
you write letters to yourself,
paper and pens are your community
because you're all alone like me.
So why don't we be alone together?

It seems silly now but
at the time it made sense;
I was lonely.
And sometimes these people have a wisdom.

I felt all of him going through me
like rain, like a team of detectives
leaving every surface dripping,

When I looked at his face again
it was me: my face my nose my lips -
he looked like he might be a relative.

I let him in.
My dog had climbed up the orange tree
and was barking. I didn't hear.

What are those? I asked gingerly.
Demons, he said.
Do demons eat dog food?

I gave him my best room,
He was always hungry
and the demons never seemed to get enough.
I went out to get clothes and food for him,
he was broken and afraid,
at night I held him as he shivered and howled,
I felt like a giant mother
I felt invincible
I felt like I was really helping someone.

It was only supposed to be for a few days
or until he found his own place
but time passed and he did not.

He was very sensitive and allergic
cleaning liquids contain toxins so those had to go.
The mop made the demons skittish so
that went too. The house got filthy.
I had to take out the books and flowers,
we bricked up the window
because he was scared of robbers.

The demons moved into the lounge and
soiled my nice carpets.
They whined and snarled and the three-headed one was
relentless, busy chewing, biting and barking all
at the same time.

Eventually I felt kind of bored and pissed off
but I couldn't remember what life was like before he came.
He lay in my best bed in my best room and
GREW
and GREW
and GREW

till there was no space for me and I had to move to
my dog's kennel, just outside the back door.

The kennel's not bad. I like animals so
I'd kitted it out quite well. A good, thick cushion and lots
of blankets for cold nights. But with the two of us it was a
little crowded. Did I mention that my dog is a Maltese?

II

From a faraway place I heard knocking.
In the dream I told myself
it can't be for me,
nobody comes to see me anymore,
they're afraid of the demons and
our conversations
don't have enough room to play,
so
I can keep dreaming this wonderful dream
where I stand thigh deep in turquoise water:
I can see the depths, but I am safe.

I wake up, fold the dog blanket and stretch.

And the knocking comes again.

I peer around the corner of the house, and by the gate I see
a man, not very old, the red-white beads of the sangoma
snug around his brown neck, and under his faded Omo t-shirt,
sticking out of his black/red/white wrap
a python skin as thick as my leg.

I smell imphephu first, then see his mild eyes.
Madam, have you seen your heart lately?

I think about it. What an odd question, but
No, I haven't. Where is my heart?
My mind flies back to a day
some months (or was it years) ago
when a stranger came to my door
with demons at his heels
and my heart ran up a tree, terrified. It stayed nearby for days

like the time when I moved in, and my cat
hid in the cellar. My heart followed the cat,
beating bravely in the darkness, then fled.
No, I haven't seen my heart for some time now.
The sage continues:
Your heart lies in a box three cities from here.
Take the 5:40 train to the third city and disembark.
You'll find you're the only one on the platform.
Fluorescent lights illuminate the grimy concrete.
Below the third light (which is flickering and about to die)
you'll find a woman selling cupfuls of peanuts.
buy them, they will be your dinner. She will ask you where you
sleep, tell her you do not know and
she will lift up her apron and you will enter
the portal of her thighs.
This is your mother.
You will not sleep well between those columns
but it won't be worse than where you've been –
in a dog house, I understand? She will tell you
where to go next.

I turn away from him and all the smells of him,
the snake is now alive and smiling.
I wasn't raised a Christian
and perhaps that's why I don't mind
taking advice from a man wearing a serpent.

III

Inside my mother's womb I lie about
the velvet lounge suite, flipping through
possible futures like magazines.
Soon Nature will force truth out of me.
like shock, and I will find myself on a landfill,
and with a strength I didn't know I possessed
I will pick up a rusting fridge and dig through
piles of rotten food and waste until
I find the Adidas shoe box that
contains my heart. I will strap it on to my wrist
and listen to its heavy tock, and I will look around
and notice the tattered women digging all around
me, and I will hear all the ticking and the tocking
of all the buried hearts, and I will wave and walk back
to the station, and under the biological clock
of city number two
I don't why
my body will just want to make babies
and clothe them in the lost sheaths
of families, when I return home
there will be no-one there:
my visitor will have left.
Flip.

IV
My boxed heart is unburied,
I clean the house, unbrick the window,
burn impephu and wait:

I am here for you
to manifest the next possibility.

I guess it doesn't get better than this
because can one never improve on
freedom.

Song of the dead

Pity the man who fell down in the marketplace,
arrested by death in the bright of day. Innocent,
condemned to the common law of fate:
pity the man.
Pity the man.

Life is just a shelter for the soul.
Life is just a shelter for the soul.

Pity the daughter in the white room, who left her
illness in the envelope of her flesh. We,
the living, she
the bereft:
pity the daughter.
Pity the daughter.

Life is just a shelter for the soul.
Life is just a shelter for the soul.

Shacks collapse and mansions fall
but each time a baby's born
a spirit comes in from the cold

Pity the dead, their privacy made public
by the absence
of their breath.
Pity the living:
the thin fabric of life just a tear away
from death.

Life is just a shelter for the soul.
Life is just a shelter…

Switching on the light

Words are building blocks,
climbing frames,
creating sentences for fearless
bodies hanging upside down.

Words. The teeth of a hungry mouth.
We are their servants, they are our tools, they
make us and unmake us, and sometimes
mistake us. They
fly out of us like swarms
of galaxies, like storms and possibilities. We
can't find the ones we need
when we need them most.

Words are fish. They nibble
at our nipples and tickle
our clitori and we scrabble for the right one to
describe
the absoluteness, the this-ness of this…
Words can only point and stare
like poor relations at a three-day feast,
like ushers at an all-night movie
showing us our seat.

They can only witness
the greedy force of life: they avert
their little beady eyes as we get on
with living it.

Words give a shape to pain
so that we can find a place
to put it. In the darkness of forgetting,
words switch on
the light.

Anthem

Words sketch images on the air.
Voice sets them on fire. I watch traditions
foot stamping, dancing themselves
back to divinity
singing that old song
that we all know as freedom
and a heavy flood bursts
between the chambers of my heart
bright red   vital...

I am alive:
my heart the same size as this fist and I
as little as this finger. We are all connected,
the living and the dead.
We arrive in life and then it
walks away from us;
leaving our bones behind
and our minds are as wide as the universe.
Human evolution began in this corner of the earth,
our ancestors left their dust as chromosomes
in each of us, they made a home,
and hominids stood up as humans and walked
languages fell out of our mouths and talked, walked their way
into and out of landscapes, mindscapes.
We walk in words, creating as we need:
we stand shadow-thin
and then
we chase the horizon   disappearing
until   we appear again.

Miracles exist. Victims become heroes:
a man with no legs is the fastest runner in the world.
a woman who could not walk swam to golden glory.
Our brains are two halves, reflecting duality,
a system of thinking
in pairs of opposites
like an on-off switch:
like a two way street:
day night wrong right man woman black white
Caster Semenya the intersex athlete
is an invitation
to consider the end of two-way thinking. A provocation
to refine our definition of what it means to be human
or woman. A conundrum. We find ourselves in a hard land
that we don't understand, we've never been here before but
this is what the future looks like. We will have to
stretch our minds from a street
to a field to an ocean to a universe to
accommodate our infinite uniqueness.

Miracles exist; we carve them out of our bodies,
we hammer them out of stone and copper,
we weave them out of desire:
for what the world does not contain
our minds create a home, as long as
we are alive,
our hearts as big as our fists and we
as little as our fingers. We are all connected
the living and the dead,
and our minds
are as wide
as the universe.

The quiet conversation

Old couple on a Havana stoep –
between the two of them, no more
the lightning-charged current of hungry
flesh seeking heat,
his torpedo desire aimed at
her, willing target,
him, joyful quarry
in the snare of her thighs;
no more the electricity of expectation.

The children of their whispered desire
are tongues of history, shared struggles
for lucidity, clear-eyed young life
sown into the furrow of humanity;
they have created four languages
to populate the world dictionary of love.

Even if the mind forgets,
the skin remembers:
the organs keep a record of their guests.
the womb carries photographs of all
her soul's passengers; this man, the
sun of his every day, this woman his
earth, his hope, his rest.

These days they sit together,
this man, this woman
who have spent so many words
on one another that now,
they are paupers
in their rich
intimacy.

Trance

(for O.M.S.)

Havana is a sunken galleon,
its people, treasure:
shoals of quick silver fish,
once captured souls, now freed
by the wrecking of the imperial flotilla.

The waves of the beach sing
conquer, surrender,
conquer, surrender,
conquer, surrender...

The moon on the waves sings
surrender, conquer,
surrender, conquer,
surrender, conquer...

... and a black man stands
10 000 miles from his ancestors,
in white cotton pyjamas,
ankle-deep in ocean whispers,
inhaling wonder;
he surrenders
to the captive beauty
of this moment,
he surrenders
to the history
that washed him up here:
triumphant
he exhales
another poem.

Breastsummer

For S.H.P.

At first I barely noticed you:
the darker skin,
the double kiss of nipples,
dot   dot
adorning the free state
of my flat brown
little-girl body.

Like buds that swell in spring,
my body opened, a flower –
handfuls ripened to cupfuls,
then the full bounty
of my own, home-grown
life support system
ran over,
a breastsummer,
showcasing potential
suitors collected like coats and shoes,

I wore their eyes,
accessorized my self-esteem.

Only, in a mirror framed by shame
I named you: inadequate
uneven
too big
too small
ugly.

This body curves
around creation,
it is the work of mighty nature.
It is my land:
I live here.
I rename the elements these days;
I farm in phrases:
beautiful, holy, vital, divine,
warm, fertile, nurturing, mine.

Sky-seasons pass and I keep turning
the sweet earth,
planting hope in even furrows,
savouring the harvest.

The organ of love

For the lover,
the most important organ
isn't what you would imagine.
For when wine is tippled, and the body
tensed for the sweet and longed-for
release,
and lips are moistened, and hair
and skin and eyes are tantalized and teased;
the nipples standing
at attention for the flight, and the seismic
ripples of the orgasm are built
to thundering height,
spare a thought for that organ
holding fate in its humble ways –

for love depends on the tongue's performance:
on what it does, and what it says.

All doors

I'm all doors:
wood creaking, swollen by moisture,
rusting metal leaking light.
At your feet my hessian
welcome smiles;
let's see how persistent you are at entering.

Just beyond reception/skin,
a guard will check your credentials,
and then you see
behind their wooden lids
the prospect of my eyes.

My lips/peeling paint   metal garage door
rolled up   reveals
a supple tongue; (a red racing car
with dodgy brakes)
with enough fuel to drive us to the end of wanting
and carry our singing souls into the platteland of imagination.
(she'll be coming round the mountain when she)
squealing with fear, we
take the midnight highway of flight.
(Wee, wee, wee, wee, all the way home)
Or lull you off with a mang wan'em pulele, ke nwela ke pula.

Walk through me to find yourself
in front of another door:
beyond this, there is always one more.

Red apples
(for Professor Keorapetse Kgositsile on his 70th birthday)

I have prayed for you,
asking you to manifest, to become part
of me, and also wished
that if you are more than a spirit,
if you possess a body also,
for you to be protected.

I didn't know you before
I saw you, I was unable to imagine what I wanted,
but when I met you I knew you were
mine. You are everybody's child,
you stand at the intersection of
will and destiny. There is enough of you
for everyone who wants.

You are a story,
a photograph,
an album of possibilities
looped like a memory
always beginning.

A small boy shakes a mossy tree
laden with ripe red
apples;
as birds throw
scraps of sweetness
through the air, and bees
bend their knees to pray to the
flower god,
and streets lay their feet in the

bucket of the sunset,
and aching dust floats off them,
and the day sighs and its jazz,
you are the deep blue night, die verlore nag,
torn away from the stars,
saxophones run down the railway tracks,
playing catch with your fears;
pennywhistle cupids shoot hearts
with melodic arrows, and honesty
can't sleep while injustice creeps along
slimy tunnels, looking for outlets;
and the boy under the bearded tree
thoughtfully collects this careless, leaping life,
his century, his day, his apples,
harvested in
the belly of his red, red shirt:

time flows downstream
and life swims hard against the flow
you are part of me now and I can stop praying
or rather, the prayer
can now become
a song,

Boy, apples, city or jazz,
wherever you are,
whoever you are,
you are enough.

Biscuit

My rural cousin's labia
were round and thick, her teenage sex
dusted by tiny curls.

I watched her body
when we bathed together –
a six-year old with eyes like ants,
storing sweetness
in the convoluted corridors of my hungry little brain.

She was dark brown
like the chocolate biscuits you got if you were
lucky after Sunday school;
after the dry weeping of Cardboard Jesus when
they let the children out
to plastic cups of Oros and one biscuit each
from the Bakers Assorted.

Among the pink wafers and lemon creams and
shortbread, the rare
delicious chocolate.

I would pounce discreetly and then turn away
to eat. First I'd nibble the edges, then
pull it apart
to find the seam of sweet gum that held
the two halves together, lick it
until it dissolved;
me and the biscuit were one: holy communion.

We girls were promised nothing but
the protection of marriage to keep
the secret at our middle sweet.

At sixteen I stopped going to church. I had to admit
that I was only there for the biscuits.

Muse

I said to my muse: you never do anything around this place.
She was lying in bed reading poetry. I said
other muses carry water from over two kilometres away.

She asked me to make her a cup of tea.
From the kitchen I shouted: Do you want a biscuit with that?
She said no. She's not greedy or excessive and she tells me

at least twice a day that she loves me. But I can't help feeling
that she's taking advantage somehow.
It's hard to get good help these days.

In the middle of the night
I find her pacing the house
and I say to her, why don't you come back to bed

and she says: shhh..... can't you hear the leaves making love
the heavy heartbeat of the buildings?
There's a crane with its fingers in the mountain's purse...

And I pause
but all I can hear is her breathing
and all I can see is the city surging

surprised
in the reflection
of her headlamp eyes.

The banquet

For some people
love is delivered
fresh from the oven,
aromatic as a prayer,
to be consumed only
after a ritualized
washing of hands.
Others meet God five
times a day:
each time they are hungry
God manifests on a plate
to fill them up.
This banquet is beyond religion,
more personal than breath,
universal.
The spent soul is replenished
through the echoing chamber
of an empty, grateful body,
each of its cells saying
repeatedly
thank you.
Thank you.
Thank you

The giver

Now, I am old:
I am no longer the quick, eager river that
rushed towards
the edge,
hungering for the giddy pleasure of
falling.

No longer the succulent grape, aching
to be pressed to release
my juice.
Neither am I the nun,
maturing in slow solitude
in an oak fortress of chastity.

These days,
I meander slowly through sunlit fields,
reflecting cloudshadow
and depositing my silten gifts in the fields of wishes
that men have carved beside me.

I am all colours of life, spread across the tongue;
like a forgotten language
now, suddenly remembered.

Acknowledgements:

Firstly to my son, for his patience and forbearance in having an absent mother whilst I was writing this book, and his father Francois for always holding the baby. This book would never have seen the light of day if it weren't for the long conversations with: Pervaiz Khan, Myesha Jenkins, Khosi Xaba, Lesley Perkes, Napo Masheane and Lebo Mashile, who always challenge, encourage, support and criticize me. I am especially indebted to Khosi for her meticulous notes on the initial manuscript, and her generous gifts of poetry and poetry-related articles.

Poets do not live by lines alone, and I thank Sarah Davids, Helen Macdonald, Pervaiz Khan and Martha Mahlangu for feeding me and making sure that I don't go out 'dressed like that!' whilst my brain is busy with other priorities. Keorapetse Kgositsile, who with his disputatious loquacity, is an honorary woman, kindly waxed the moustache of 'Stolen Rivers', making it more beautiful.

Some of the poems were previously published in these journals: *Poui: Cave Hill Journal, Botsotso, A Hudson View, Canopic Jar* and *Shine e-journals*. 'Origin' and 'The quiet conversation' appeared in *We Are!* (Penguin, 2008). Thanks to the editors and publishers who continue to provide platforms for new poets.

'Anthem' and 'What the Dead Say' were commissioned by Apples and Snakes for a chapbook for UK tour (2009) and 'The Giver' was part of a series of poems commissioned by Dion | Chang's *Flux Trends*.

Many of these poems arrived or were polished during a one-month residency at Villa Hellebosch, a magnificent writers retreat managed by Belgian writers' organization, Het Beschrijf in March 2009, I would like to thank Alexandre Cool for her hospitality, and Ismael Mohamed of the National Arts Festival in Grahamstown for creating new opportunities for SA writers.

I gratefully acknowledge Margaret Busby, who wrote such a generous foreword and gave valuable advice in the making of the book, and my publisher, Colleen Higgs, who encouraged me to publish *Taller than Buildings*, and is now adopting this baby too. This beautiful book was insightfully edited by Angela Voges and beautifully designed by Jacqui Stecher.

Other Poetry titles by Modjaji Books

Fourth Child by Megan Hall

Life in Translation by Azila Talit Reisenberger

Please, Take Photographs by Sindiwe Magona

Burnt Offering by Joan Metelerkamp

Strange Fruit by Helen Moffett

Oleander by Fiona Zerbst

Invisible Earthquake:
A woman's journal through stillbirth
by Malika Ndlovu